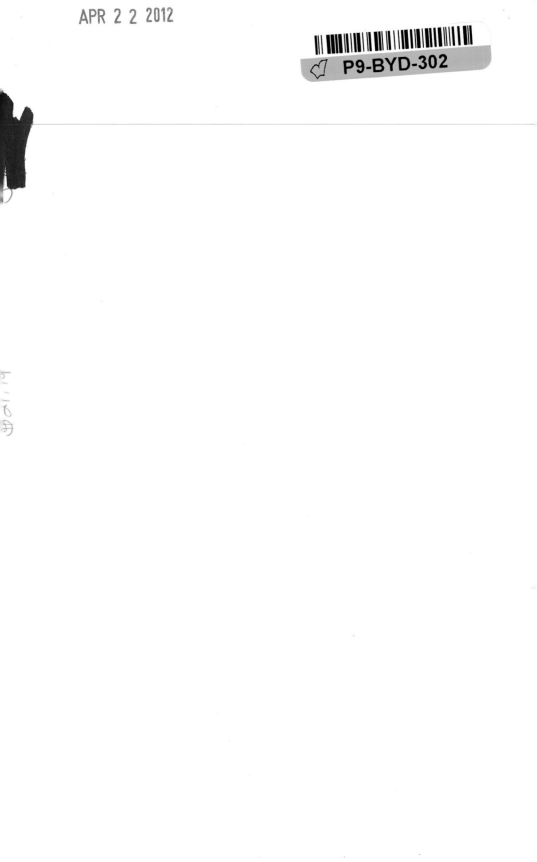

P9-BYD-302

VELOCITY

THE FASCINATING, FANTASTIC

UNUSUAL HISTORY OF ROBOTS

BY SEAN McCOLLUM

i-SOBOT

Content Consultant: Seth Hutchinson, PhD
Professor of Electrical and Computer Engineering
University of Illinois, Champaign, Illinois

CAPSTONE PRESS
a capstone imprint

Velocity is published by Capstone Press,
151 Good Counsel Drive, P.O. Box 669, Mankato, Minnesota 56002.
www.capstonepub.com

Books published by Capstone Press are manufactured with paper
containing at least 10 percent post-consumer waste.

McCollum, Sean.
   The fascinating, fantastic, unusual history of robots/by Sean McCollum.
      p. cm.—(Velocity. unusual histories)
   Includes bibliographical references and index.
   Summary: "Traces the history of robots, from the early designs of the mid–1900s to
today's modern designs"—Provided by publisher.
   ISBN 978-1-4296-5490-6 (library binding) 1. Robots—History—Juvenile literature. I.
Title.
   TJ211.2.M376 2012
   629.8'9209—dc22   2010049201

Editorial Credits: Pam Mamsch
Art Director: Suzan Kadribasic
Designers: Deepika Verma, Jasmeen Kaur, Yasin Khan

Photo Credits
Alamy: Photos 12, 9, 11 (bottom left), 42, Mary Evans Picture Library, 10, Broccoli Photography,
11 (top), Pictorial Press Ltd, 11 (bottom right), Alan Gallery, 12, The Print Collector, 13 (bottom),
Andrew Linscott, 22 (top), PHOTOTAKE Inc., 23, AF Archive, 36, Jeremy Sutton-Hibbert,
40; AP Images: David Parry/PA Wire, 37 (bottom), Dima Gavrysh, 41; Bridgman Art Library:
Museo Archeologico, Bari, Italy, 8; Corbis: Mike Powell, 21 (top); Courtesy of Allen Vanguard: 32;
Courtesy of the Computer History Museum: Mark Richards, 17; Getty Images: Toru Yamanaka/
AFP, 1, 6, Yoshikazu Tsuno/AFP, 4, 38, 45, Toshifumi Kitamura/AFP, 5, PhotoQuest, 13 (top),
SSPL, 14 (top), Larry Burrows/Time & Life Pictures, 14 (bottom), Claudio Edinger, 15, Jack
Guez/AFP, 33; Istockphoto: Gerenme, 18-19, mbbirdy, 37 (top); NASA: 24-25, JPL, 25 (front),
28; National Archives and Records Administration: Conseil Régional de Basse-Normandie, 30;
Photolibrary: Maximilian Stock LTD/SPL, 20-21; Rex USA: Masatoshi Okauchi, cover, Alex
Lentati/Evening Standard, 35 (bottom); Science Photo Library: Sam Ogden, 44; Shutterstock:
Neliyana Kostadinova, cover (background), Rainer Plendl, 7 (top), Joe White, 16 (top), SPbPhoto,
16 (bottom); Small World News Service: 39; Stanford University: Stanford Racing, 7 (bottom);
Swarm-bots: www.swarm-bots.org/Ecole Polytechnique Fédérale de Lausanne, 29; U.S. Air Force:
Staff Sgt. Brian Ferguson, 31; U.S. NAVY: Photographer's Mate 2nd Class Richard J. Brunson, 27;
Wikipedia: U.S. Marine Corps/Lance Cpl. M. L. Meier, 34-35; www.CartoonStock.com: 43.

Printed in the United States of America in Melrose Park, Illinois.
032011   006112LKF11

TABLE OF CONTENTS

INTRODUCTION
What is a Robot? 4

CHAPTER 1
Dreams of Mechanical Beings 8

CHAPTER 2
Computers: Robots Get a Brain 12

CHAPTER 3
Robots go to Work 18

CHAPTER 4
Robot Risk Takers 24

CHAPTER 5
Robots in the Ranks 30

CHAPTER 6
Robots at Home and Play 36

CHAPTER 7
The Future: Will Robots Ever Learn? 42

Glossary 46
Read More 47
Internet Sites 47
Index 48

What is a Robot?

The curtains slid back. Cameras flashed, and reporters whispered. Something strange walked out. It looked like a young woman, but there was something weird about her.

The eyes blinked. Then it spoke. "Hello everybody. I am cybernetic human HRP-4C," it said. It crossed its long, rubbery hands. A whirring noise came from the shiny plastic body as it bowed.

HRP-4C was introduced to the public in March 2009.

Each year, scientists and engineers power up a new generation of **humanoids**. These robots are getting more lifelike every year. Their bodies move more gracefully. They recognize faces and voices. They can sense touch. Humanoids answer questions and express emotion. They can perform these actions with less and less human control.

HRP-2 is an ancestor of the HRP-4C.

For many people, humanoids like HRP-4C are science fiction becoming reality. Humanlike machines are a common dream of what robots should be. But what exactly is a robot? That is a tricky question. Even robot engineer Joseph Engelberger struggled to answer it. "I can't define a robot, but I know one when I see one," he said.

humanoid—a robot that has a human shape or characteristics

Kinds of Robots

Robots can be divided into three main categories. These categories depend on the amount of human control needed to operate the robot.

Teleoperated robots: Humans operate these robots by remote control. A person gives electronic commands while the robot performs them. A remote-control car is an example of a teleoperated robot.

Supervisory robots: Humans program this kind of robot to do a certain job. The robot then completes the task on its own. This kind of robot is common in factories.

robots in a car assembly plant

Autonomous robots: These robots are designed to work with little or no human input.

Stanley was built by the Stanford Racing team and won the DARPA Grand Challenge race for autonomous robots in 2005.

Robots are becoming more useful every year. Most are put to work in factories building cars and other products. Some explore deep space or ocean depths. Others help doctors perform surgery. Some even scout battlefields and search disaster sites. These machines help us tackle many dull and dangerous jobs. Some even entertain us with tricks and dance steps.

Robots began as an idea in people's imaginations long ago. Now their electronic brains and bodies are helping create the future.

autonomous—capable of moving or working independently

Chapter 1

Dreams of Mechanical Beings

The idea of mechanical beings has been around for hundreds of years. Ancient thinkers imagined smart machines that could work with little human control. Hephaestus is the Greek god of fire, metal, and technology. According to a Greek myth, he built a giant security guard named Talos out of bronze. Talos circled the island of Crete three times a day. He was powerful and dangerous. His job was to drive off or crush invaders.

Talos is shown on this ancient vase.

Some early inventors worked to turn ideas into real machines. They played around with springs, gears, and other mechanical parts. These mechanical creatures are known as **automatons**. Most automatons can only perform a trick or two. They are more like toys than robots.

de Vaucanson's duck

Frenchman Jacques de Vaucanson built several automatons in the 1700s. The first was a flute player. By adjusting pegs on a tube, the fake flutist could be programmed to play 12 different songs.

Another triumph was his mechanical duck. It stood, sat, and flapped its wings. It could pluck corn out of a bowl of water and lift its head to swallow. It even pooped!

automaton—an automatic machine

Automatic Machines

The textile, or fabric weaving, industry was the first to use mass **automation**. Automatic looms, or weaving machines, read paper cards punched with holes. The cards gave commands for what to weave. These machines worked faster than humans. They also made fewer mistakes.

Engineers invented many new and better machines from the late 1700s through about 1900. This period became known as the Industrial Revolution. By about 1900, people had also discovered ways to more easily produce and control electricity.

Robots still only existed in people's imaginations. But the pieces were coming together to make them possible.

Robots Get Their Name

In 1921 the word "robot" first appeared in the play *R.U.R. (Rossum's Universal Robots)*. It was written by Czech writer Karel Capek. The story is about mechanical workers that rise up and wipe out their human masters. In the end, two of the robots develop humanlike feelings.

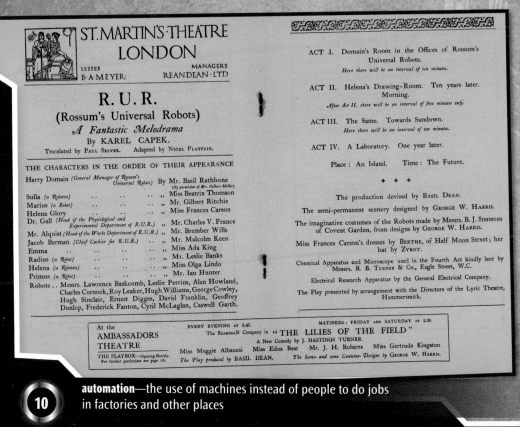

automation—the use of machines instead of people to do jobs in factories and other places

Robots have been a favorite subject of books and movies. Whether good or evil, they bring excitement to science fiction.

Heroes

R2-D2 and C-3PO—*Star Wars* droids that come to the rescue time after time

Wall-E—quirky clean-up robot from *Wall-E* movie; helps bring humans back to Earth

Autobots—good, shape-shifting robots from *Transformers*

Villains

Terminators—killer androids from *The Terminator* movies

Decepticons—destructive shape-shifting robots from *Transformers*

Wall-E

a Terminator

C-3PO

FACT:

The word *robota* means "forced labor" in Czech. Karel credited his brother Josef with thinking up the term for the mechanical workers in the play.

Chapter 2

Computers: Robots Get a Brain

Engineers had the knowledge to invent and build electronic gadgets by the mid-1900s. Robots, however, were still missing a system that could control their actions. Computers began to answer that need.

Today's powerful laptops are thinner than some books and weigh just a few pounds. They can handle huge amounts of information and make millions of decisions per second. Such a machine was difficult to imagine in the 1930s.

Alan Turing: The Man Who Imagined Computers

British mathematician Alan Turing (1912–1954) helped make computers a reality. In 1936 Turing began writing down his ideas for a new kind of machine. The machine would use mathematical logic to figure out problems. Several years passed before his concepts could be tested in a real machine.

FACT:

Turing's talent for math and logic also played a key role during World War II (1939–1945). He cracked the top-secret code used by Nazi Germany. This gave the British, Americans, and other allies a big advantage.

a sculpture of Alan Turing

The First HUGE Computers

Work is completed on the Harvard Mark I computer.

The earliest computers were huge. The Harvard Mark I was completed in 1944. One of the first **digital** computers, it was 51 feet (15.5 meters) long and weighed 10,000 pounds (4,536 kilograms). It used 500 miles (805 kilometers) of wire. This big machine helped scientists quickly solve difficult math problems. Computer engineers began programming computers to do tasks other than calculations by the early 1950s.

FACT:

Charles Babbage was an English mathematician and inventor. In the 1820s, he drew up plans for what he called a Difference Engine. This machine was powered by a crank. It could calculate large numbers. It is considered an early kind of computer.

digital—related to using numerical codes to represent words, pictures, and other data

Elmer and Elsie

Dr. William Grey Walter

one of Walter's tortoise robots

Dr. William Grey Walter conducted some interesting experiments in 1948 and 1949. He added light sensors to two simple electronic machines on wheels. He called them tortoises because of their shape. They were named Elmer and Elsie.

Walter did not program these robots to do specific tasks. Instead, he programmed them to follow two basic commands:

1) back up if something blocked them
2) go toward light

He was surprised and amused by how they behaved. They acted almost like animals exploring territory. Elmer and Elsie are two of the earliest autonomous robots.

ISAAC ASIMOV

Isaac Asimov (1920–1992) loved science. He wrote more than 200 science fiction books. Robots often appeared in his stories, such as *Little Lost Robot*, *The Bicentennial Man*, and *I, Robot*.

One of his favorite themes was the idea that robots might become self-aware. He liked to explore what would happen if they could learn, create, and experience emotions. This idea has become a favorite feature in science fiction robots.

Isaac Asimov

Let's Get Small

Switching devices are what make computers compute. These switches can be either open or closed, like an on/off light switch. Open switches represent the value "false." Closed switches represent the value "true." The computer links these switches to make an electronic code that can do calculations and run programs. The more switches, the better and faster the computer.

Dr. Walter's robots and most early computers used glass vacuum tubes for switching. Like lightbulbs, vacuum tubes were fragile and frequently burned out. Each vacuum tube could handle only one open/closed task.

In 1958 electronics engineers Jack Kilby and Robert Noyce each invented an integrated circuit. This **microchip** eventually contained multiple transistors that took up little space. Computers were getting smaller and more powerful at the same time. This advancement was a big leap for robotics.

FACT:

Today's microchips can contain millions of **transistors**.

microchips

glass vacuum tubes

---

transistor—a very small part that acts like a switch and controls electrical current in a device

microchip—a series of electronic circuits built into a thin piece of silicon or similar material

Shakey Rolls

The Artificial Intelligence Center at Stanford Research Institute introduced Shakey in 1969. This robot looked like an air conditioner on wheels. It was programmed to steer its way around obstacles or to move them. Bump detectors and a range finder helped Shakey "see" its path.

It took hours for Shakey's computer program to figure out a course across a room. Still, this machine was a breakthrough. *Life* magazine called Shakey the "first electronic person." Robots now had a kind of brain—a computer.

range finder

television camera

on-board logic

camera control unit

bump detector

drive wheel

drive motor

Chapter 3

Robots go to Work

In 1956 inventor George Devol met with engineer Joseph Engelberger. Devol had an idea for a kind of mechanical arm. He was not sure how useful it would be. The two men put their ideas together and created the first robotics company, Unimation Inc. In 1961 the company installed the first robot at a General Motors car plant. Called Unimate, the robot was a big, strong arm. It could rotate, grab, and lift. Its first job was to stack hot metal plates. Unimates were soon programmed to do welding and other tasks.

a robot welding auto parts

Industrial robots quickly proved their worth. Since the 1960s, robotic arms have elbowed their way into many jobs on car assembly lines. They are perfect for dull, dangerous, and dirty jobs. They aren't multi-talented like human workers. They can only do simple tasks. But they don't grow bored, tired, or grumpy like humans might.

Industrial robots work with **precision**. They can weld a spot in the exact location pinpointed by their programming. They can tighten a bolt the perfect number of turns. They can do the same task perfectly each and every time.

precision—the quality of being highly accurate or exact

Modern Robots on the Job

Assembly robots have become important machines in high-tech industries. The parts in computers and electronics have grown smaller and smaller. Nimble robot "fingers" are good for handling microchips and other tiny parts.

Some big warehouses now use robotic forklifts to get products and load them onto trucks. Some of these Automatic Guided Vehicles (AGVs) sense wires in the floor and follow them. Laser Guided Vehicles (LGVs) use lasers to know where to go. Laser scanners help these carts avoid crashing into, or running over, human workers.

FACT:

The Port of Rotterdam in the Netherlands employs more than 100 robotic AGVs and cargo-loading cranes. These powerful rolling robots help load and unload ships.

AGVs at work

a technician works on a robot

ROBOT COWORKERS

So far, most robots have taken over tasks that need little skill or training. As robots become more advanced, companies will find more uses for them. Studying to become a computer programmer or robot repair technician could be a very smart career choice for the future.

Robots
on the
Farm

Improved sensors and more computer power let robots pitch in with farm work. Robotic machines feed and milk cows on some dairy farms. Cows enter a stall where a robot automatically hooks up pumps to the cows' udders.

Fruit-picking robots will soon arrive in orange and apple orchards. One robotics company is developing a two-part system. One robot will scan the tree and spot all the fruit. Then its partner will come along and do the picking with its eight long arms.

model of a
fruit-picking robot

ROBOT DOCS

Robots are making the rounds at some hospitals. The InTouch Robot lets doctors examine patients from halfway around the world. Using a camera and joystick, the doctor steers the robot into a patient's room. The doctor's face appears on a screen. He can ask questions and find out how the patient is doing.

Robots are even helping doctors do surgery. The da Vinci Surgical System lets surgeons work inside a patient through small slits in the skin. The surgeon controls robotic arms that can see, grab, and cut with precision. Robot surgery is now the preferred choice for some kinds of operations.

FACT:

Medical researchers are developing microbots. These robots will be tiny enough to move through blood vessels to hunt for health problems.

The da Vinci robot system is used by surgeons.

Chapter 4

Robot Risk Takers

The *Cassini* orbiter was sent to explore Saturn in 1997. It carried the *Huygens* robot probe.

In 1969 Neil Armstrong was the first human to set foot on the moon. But he was not the first visitor from Earth. Ten years earlier, a robot **probe** launched by scientists in the Soviet Union had landed on the lunar surface. The Soviet Union and the United States launched dozens of robotic explorers in the 1960s. These machines sent back information that helped make it possible for humans to land on the moon.

Robots are perfect explorers for dangerous missions. They don't panic. They do not freeze to death or need oxygen to survive. No hearts are broken if they break down, disappear, or blow up. They can explore without risking human life.

probe—a tool or device that explores something and sends back information

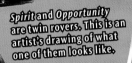

Spirit and Opportunity are twin rovers. This is an artist's drawing of what one of them looks like.

ROLLING AROUND MARS

The National Aeronautics and Space Administration (NASA) landed twin rovers on the surface of Mars in 2004. They were named *Spirit* and *Opportunity*. These six-wheeled robots slowly rolled across miles of Martian soil. Scientists on Earth sent commands that told the rovers where to go and what to investigate.

Explorers
of the Seas

Robotic probes have sailed the seas since the 1950s. Remotely operated vehicles (ROVs) are piloted by remote control. They can be as small as a small dog or as big as an elephant. A cable attaches an ROV to a surface ship or submarine. These robots can dive to depths that are deadly for human divers and dangerous for minisubs. They have explored the ocean floor and helped track down lost shipwrecks, such as the *Titanic*.

an ROV

FACT:

Volcano researchers sometimes send robots to explore active volcanoes. These robots check for dangerous gases and collect soil samples. They can alert scientists that an eruption may be coming.

Autonomous underwater vehicles (AUVs) don't need human operators. These torpedo-shaped robots can guide themselves. AUVs cruise through the water and collect data. They measure depths, ocean currents, and water temperatures. They also provide accurate maps of the sea floor. Sometimes called gliders, AUVs use very little power and can recharge their own batteries. This feature allows them to stay at sea for weeks or months. In 2009 the glider RU-27 was the first robot to cross the Atlantic Ocean by itself. It took 221 days to make the voyage from New Jersey to Spain.

an autonomous underwater vehicle.

Robots to the Rescue

Since the 1990s, some robot explorers have been programmed to scope out disaster areas that are too dangerous for human rescuers. These robots have proven especially useful when disasters like earthquakes or storms cause buildings to collapse. They can drive or crawl inside wreckage to search for survivors. Most carry cameras that send images back to rescue workers. Others have sensors that sniff out bombs or dangerous chemicals.

Urbie, a search-and-rescue robot

Search-and-rescue robots come in all shapes and designs. One small tank-shaped robot is called Urbie. It can roll over rocks and up steps to scout situations. Humans can use the information Urbie gathers to come up with rescue plans. Another rescue robot looks and moves like a snake. This movement allows it to slither through tiny openings that might block Urbie and other bigger robots.

Swarmbots

Swarmbots will soon join the search party, though they are still in development. These robots work as a team. Dozens can be sent into a building. They spread out and communicate. They quickly map an area and report what they find to one another.

Swarmbots have a big advantage over other robots. If one of these small machines is damaged or destroyed, the others keep scrambling to do their job. Swarmbots may even link together to tackle a task too big for a single Swarmbot.

Swarmbots

FACT:

Scientists who develop swarm robots use their knowledge of how swarms of insects, such

Chapter 5

Robots in the Ranks

Militaries are sending more robots into combat every year. Like robot explorers, these machines take on deadly jobs. They can also be turned into killers.

Military planners have worked for a long time to put robots on battlefields. During World War II, the German army used crawling bombs. They were called Goliaths. The minitanks rolled toward enemy lines, then blew up.

Goliaths were crawling bombs used by the Germans during World War II.

FACT:
The Predator UAV can stay in the air for up to 20 hours.

Predator in the Sky

Robot fighters really took off in the 1990s. In 1995, the U.S. Air Force sent the Predator unmanned aerial vehicle (UAV) into the air for the first time. A pilot on the ground flies the aircraft by remote control.

At first, the Predator was used only for scouting. It spied from above and radioed the information back to base. More recently, the United States has armed a new model with missiles. The Reaper searches for the enemy. Once a target is spotted, the pilot on the ground fires the missiles.

Almost 7,000 Predators and Reapers were flying military missions by 2010. The U.S. military plans to replace 30 percent of its soldiers, sailors, and pilots with robots by the year 2020.

'Bots on the Ground

a Defender ROV bomb disposal robot

Since the 1980s, engineers have tried designing military robots for duty on the ground. Successes include robot bomb disposal units. They can tackle the dangerous job of disarming bombs. These teleoperated robots have seen a lot of action in the wars in Iraq and Afghanistan.

SHOULD ROBOTS SHOOT?

Robots will play even bigger roles in the military in the future. They provide effective ways to patrol and scout without putting soldiers in danger. But should they ever be programmed to pull the trigger on their own?

So far, robotic weapons are almost all handled by humans using remote control. Even this raises questions. Will leaders be more likely to start wars if their country's flesh-and-blood soldiers are not at risk? Is it easier to blow up people if they are just blips on a video monitor?

an Israeli robot that shoots paint balls

RoboDog and Friends

BigDog in action

A new generation of military robots will soon join the ranks. Among them are robotic trucks to carry supplies through dangerous areas. Another freaky-looking robot goes by the name BigDog. It trots on four legs and can carry more than 300 pounds (136 kg) of equipment and supplies. It can run over very rough ground.

Other military robots are built to serve as scouts. Soldiers are already tossing the Recon Scout Throwbot through windows. Once inside a building, this two-wheeled robot can scan the scene and report danger hiding inside.

The United States and other countries are developing military robots that can attack and kill. The Talon Maars robot will be armed with machine guns. It can roll into a dangerous situation and shoot if it needs to.

Talon Maars robot

Robots at Home and Play

Rosie the Robot got a lot of people's hopes up. She served as the maid on *The Jetsons*. This cartoon first appeared in 1962. It was set in the 23rd century. The show portrayed a cool, gadget-filled world. Rosie cooked, cleaned, nagged, and kept the household running smoothly. In people's imaginations, autonomous household robots seemed only a short time away.

Rosie the Robot

The first robotic vacuum cleaner—the Electrolux Trilobite—was sold in 2001. It rolls around the carpet and floor in a pattern until it vacuums the whole room. It uses sensors to avoid obstacles and to keep it from tumbling down stairs. When its battery runs low, it searches out its recharger. Today other vacuuming robots are available as well.

Roomba vacuum robot

The technology used in the Trilobite has been adapted to other home robots. One is a robot that mops floors. Another robot works underwater to clean swimming pools. Robots that mow the lawn are available. They follow a programmed pattern, turning when they sense markers that tell them where the yard ends.

a lawn-mowing robot

The Challenge of Building Household Robots

Creating robots that help with housework such as cooking is difficult. Robots work best in places where they do the same thing again and again in a setting that never changes. But humans don't live that way. Most people are messy and unpredictable. Human behavior can confuse even the smartest robots.

The main problem has to do with robots' ability to recognize things and understand their meaning. For example, it is easy for a person to tell the difference between a box of sugar and a box of dishwasher soap. It takes a very advanced robot to do the same task.

HUMAN-ROBOT

How will humans relate to robots in the future? Will we treat them like pets? Will we order them around? Robot designers are researching these questions. They want to know what robot looks and behaviors appeal most to humans.

Researchers have made interesting discoveries about people's reactions to robots. Most humans are OK with robots that are clearly machines. They are also comfortable with humanoid robots that look like friendly cartoon characters. But they prefer robots to be smaller than they are. Most people are uncomfortable around humanoids that look and act almost human.

Jules the robot can mimic human facial expressions.

Robots to Help Humans at Home

Designing complex machines to aid people who need extra help is an exciting field in robotics. Japanese companies have taken the lead in creating many of these robot assistants. The number of elderly in that country is growing quickly. By the year 2020, one in four Japanese people will be 65 years old or older. Robots may fill a growing need for assistance.

Wakamaru, built by Mitsubishi, is a robot designed to help the elderly. This small, yellow humanoid recognizes voices and faces. It also recognizes about 10,000 words. It reminds people of appointments, or when they are supposed to take their medicine. Wakamaru will also make a phone call for help if a person falls or gets sick.

Robots for Independence

Robot assistants can help people with disabilities live more independently. My Spoon is a robot invented by Takashi Fuzawa. He injured his back and is paralyzed. He designed the machine to help feed himself.

the Power Knee wearable robot

Wearable robots also promise more mobility for people who have lost the use of their legs. ReWalk is a kind of robot called an exoskeleton. It straps to a wearer's legs and back. Buttons on a wristband command ReWalk to stand and sit. It can also walk and climb steps. The device is used with crutches for balance.

Chapter 7

The Future: Will Robots Ever Learn?

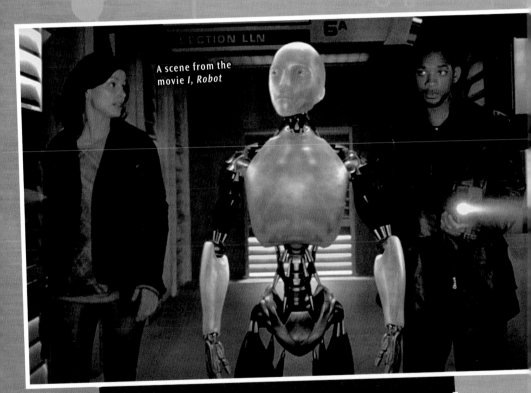

A scene from the movie *I, Robot*

SECTION LLN
6A

"What we want is a machine that can learn from experience." That was the hope of computer genius Alan Turing in the 1940s. He believed machines that could think like humans might be possible by the year 2000.

That hasn't happened yet, and might never happen. The human mind is incredibly complex. Understanding and trying to copy how it learns continues to stump robotics engineers.

Though they can't think like humans, robots can be programmed to do many things. Robotic chess players have defeated human chess champs. Factory robots can perform many jobs better than human workers.

Programming, however, has big limitations. A programmer must input every possible command into a robot's computer brain. Even small surprises can stall a robot in its tracks. Insects with tiny brains can deal with unusual situations better than most robots.

Programmers have tried to solve this problem with better sensors, faster computers, and more programming. This approach has succeeded in creating machines that can simulate thinking, or Artificial Intelligence (AI). But the hope that machines can learn on their own has yet to be fulfilled.

FACT:

Some robotics engineers are studying animals for new ideas about how to build robots. This research is called biomimetics.

The Quest for Strong AI

Some scientists wonder if robots can develop like children do, by playing and relating to the world around them. They wonder if robots could take a solution for one problem and use it to solve a different problem. For example, a robot that figures out that a key can unlock the door of a house might adapt that knowledge. Then it might use a key to unlock a car door. Robots that could learn and adapt could lead to machines that think like people. Robotics experts sometimes call this type of thinking strong artificial intelligence.

Strong artificial intelligence scares some people. They wonder if such robots would eventually reject human control and become dangerous. So far, science fiction is the only place such rebellious machines exist.

A researcher interacts with Cog, a humanoid robot

Robots in the Near Future

The field of robotics continues to introduce amazing machines. Soon doctors may send a mouse-sized robot into your belly to have a look around. A robot receptionist might recognize you and welcome you to the dentist's office. Robotic tutors may roll into your classroom and help explain algebra.

How mind-blowing will robots become? As incredible as technology and the human imagination can make them!

Qrio, a humanoid robot

artificial intelligence (ar-tih-FISH-uhl in-TEL-uh-juhnts)—the science of creating computers that can do things that previously required human intelligence

automation (aw-tuh-MAY-shuhn)—the use of machines instead of people to do jobs in factories and other places

automaton (aw-TAH-muh-tahn)—an automatic machine

autonomous (aw-TAH-nuh-muhs)—capable of moving or working independently

digital (DIH-juh-tuhl)—related to using numerical codes to represent words, pictures, and other data

humanoid (HYOO-muh-noyd)—a robot that has a human shape or characteristics

microchip (MY-kroh-chip)—a series of electronic circuits built into a thin piece of silicon or similar material

precision (prih-SI-zhuhn)—the quality of being highly accurate or exact

probe (PROHB)—a tool or device that explores something and sends back information

program (PROH-gram)—a series of instructions written in computer language that controls how a computer works

sensor (SEN-sur)—a device that can detect changes in heat, light, sound, etc. and send information to a controlling device

transistor (tran-ZISS-tur)—a very small part that acts like a switch and controls electrical current in a device

READ MORE

Domaine, Helena. *Robotics.* Cool Science. Minneapolis: Lerner Publications, 2006.

Editors of YES Magazine. *Robots: From Everyday to Out of This World.* Toronto: Kids Can Press, 2008.

Hyland, Tony. *How Robots Work.* Robots and Robotics. North Mankato, Minn.: Smart Apple Media, 2008.

Jefferis, David. *Robot Workers.* Robozones. New York: Crabtree Publishing **Company, 2007.**

INTERNET SITES

FactHound offers a safe, fun way to find Internet sites related to this book. All of the sites on FactHound have been researched by our staff.

Here's all you do:

Visit *www.facthound.com*
Type in this code: 9781429654906

artificial intelligence, 17, 43, 44
Asimov, Isaac, 15
Autobots, 11
automatic guided vehicles (AGVs), 20
automatons, 9
autonomous robots, 7, 15
autonomous underwater vehicles (AUVs), 27

Babbage, Charles, 13
BigDog, 34

C-3PO, 11
Cog, 44
Capek, Karel, 10, 11

da Vinci Surgical System, 23
de Vaucanson, Jacques, 9
Decepticons, 11
Devol, George, 18

Fuzawa, Takashi, 41

Electrolux Trilobite, 37
Elmer, 15
Elsie, 15
Engelberger, Joseph, 5, 18

Goliaths, 30

Harvard Mark I, 13
Hephaestus, 8
HRP-2, 5
HRP-4C, 4, 5
humanoids, 5, 39, 40, 44, 45

Industrial Revolution, 10
industrial robots, 19
InTouch Robot, 23

Kilby, Jack, 16

laser guided vehicles (LGVs), 20

Mars rovers, 25
medical robots, 23
microchips, 16, 20

Noyce, Robert, 16

Predator, 31
probes, 24, 26

Qrio, 45

R2-D2, 11
Reaper, 31
remotely operated vehicles (ROVs), 26, 32
ReWalk, 41

Robota, 11
Rosie the Robot, 36
Rossum's Universal Robots, 10
RU-27, 27

search-and-rescue robots, 28
Shakey, 17
supervisory robots, 7
Swarmbots, 29

Talon Maars, 35
Talos, 8
teleoperated robots, 6, 32
Terminators, 11
Turing, Alan, 12, 42

Unimate, 18
unmanned aerial vehicle (UAV), 31
Urbie, 28

Wakamaru, 40
Wall-E, 11
Walter, Dr. William Grey, 15, 16